The Dark Film

PAUL FARLEY was born in Liverpool in 1965,
and studied at the Chelsea School of Art. He has
published three previous collections with Picador,
The Boy From the Chemist is Here to See You (1998),
The Ice Age (2002) and *Tramp in Flames* (2006), and
has received many awards for his work, including
most recently the E. M. Forster Award from the
American Academy of Arts and Letters.

Paul Farley

The Dark Film

PICADOR

First published 2012 by Picador
an imprint of Pan Macmillan, a division of Macmillan Publishers Limited
Pan Macmillan, 20 New Wharf Road, London N1 9RR
Basingstoke and Oxford
Associated companies throughout the world
www.panmacmillan.com

ISBN 978-0-330-46123-8

1 3 5 7 9 8 6 4 2

A CIP catalogue record for this book is available from
the British Library.

Printed and bound by CPI Group (UK) Ltd, Croydon, CR0 4YY

for Elaine, Alison and David

Contents

The Dark Film

The Power

Forget all of that end-of-the-pier
palm-reading stuff. Picture a seaside town
in your head. Start from its salt-wrack-rotten smells
and raise the lid of the world to change the light,
then go as far as you want: the ornament
of a promenade, the brilliant greys of gulls,
the weak grip of a crane in the arcades
you've built, ballrooms to come alive at night,
then a million-starling roost, an opulent
crumbling like cake icing . . .
                              Now, bring it down
in the kind of fire that flows along ceilings,
that knows the spectral blues; that always starts
in donut fryers or boardwalk kindling
in the dead hour before dawn, that leaves pilings
marooned by mindless tides, that sends a plume
of black smoke high enough to stain the halls
of clouds. Now look around your tiny room
and tell me that you haven't got the power.

Adults

I'd look up to them looming on street corners,
or down on them at night through my bedroom blinds,
crashing home from the Labour Club, mad drunk.
After a while I decided they must be unhappy.

And this didn't tally at all with my view of their world.
Adults could float through days sole sovereigns
of everything around them, could pass through walls
of childish silence, or just take off in the *Sunbeam*.

So why did I find them at hometime slumped in their chairs
or throwing their tea up the wall? Why did they cry
on their own downstairs with the whole house listening in
or plead softly to people who weren't even there?

You think you know all the answers at that age.
You can't wait to grow up and sort them out, then go
to live in Mayfair or Singapore, wear a smoking jacket
and drink gin slings all day, like real writers do.

The New Babies

We pushed our notes through the floorboards of the house
for the future, before they moved us into the vans.
I couldn't see over the drawn up ramp,
so counted streetlamps. A wasp got into the back
where we sat on the settee and tried to play house.
A wardrobe kicked like a horse where it was lashed.
The smells – of bag-washes, alehouses, hot fat –
faded, then the road grew bumpier. We were led out.

Our tree – an ash – was hard to find for the first few weeks.
They all looked the same to me. Saying that seems
ridiculous now, but the nearest we'd ever been
to a tree was climbing the bunk ladder at bedtime.
Up the dancers! parents still said when the sun went down
and it took a while to adjust to the stork's-nest piles
each one of us took. Every night the moon would find
more chinks in the leaves as it moved across the sky.

But we settled in, and that Christmas was superb.
We decked our tree out in baubles and all our neighbours
did the same – the Pintos' oak, the McGuffies' fir –
and we all went quarters in on pigs that were slaughtered.
Spring smelled like a freshly peeled twig, and the birds
woke us up before it was light and our Dad went berserk.
I was only a slip of a kid, so could find a perch
high up in the crown and look out over the world.

All the green was breaking up and there was a haze
of woodsmoke over the clearings we couldn't help but make.
We helped our Dad knock together a new cradle.
Our tree creaked every night for a week in a gale.
Something was coming, it was plain to see in his face.
Bad dreams – of fire, of the end of the world – came
and I woke them with my cries, and owls took the blame,
but I knew that everything was about to change.

Force Field

Look at all the things I've wrapped myself inside:
Too quiet: put some tape hiss under this.
I was building a force field, as rough and ready
as sparrows wove their nests from bus tickets,
dog hair and cobwebs, what lay to hand,
though in my case, what came in through the eye
on winter evenings: spacemen who'd land
on hostile planets drew a line in the sand
to try to keep out monsters from the id;
Valve synths here, surely? Technicolor.
I walked to school dressed like the Ready Brek Kid.

Now knock it back: out-of-date Ektachrome.
The teacher took the window hook and pulled
fresh air into the classroom because we stank.
One kid hummed like Pig-Pen from Peanuts:
scribbly emanations. Another trailed
his two co-habiting wet Alsatians.
Many were starting out on Players or Woodbines
so there was that, too, and never forget
how feral life was lived then: rain and spittle,
ashes, cat's piss, crushed umbellifers . . .
16mm. Theatrical leader.
When weekly bath nights locked into alignment
their eve would muster such a thickened funk
the teachers gagged. That was the power we had.

Another thing we kept between us and the world.

Quality Street

How many other kids would turn
   themselves into a camera
replete with scrims and gels and tints
   to see the world in new colours?
Soul billows through net curtains.
   A glutton finds his favourite seat
and sets to working through a tin of Quality Street.

The wrapper of a strawberry cream
   unpeels a vivid red to dye
the evening bloody monochrome.
   Under a pre-Cambrian sky
the scale of blood and blood-shadow has made
   an ancient fortress of the maisonettes;
a dog crossing the square is flayed
    alive, leaves bloody tracks
and looks back with a blood-bright eye
   before it finds a bin-shed door
and roots the opened guts of bin liners,
   all in the light of a great fire,
and when our sun becomes a swollen core
there will be other evenings like this to endure.

But this is now, or rather, then. The gold
is taken from a toffee penny and held
   over the eyes: gold cellophane
   that makes a legend of the rain,

a sheet so small being beaten out
by greedy vision until the whole estate
turns lustrous from the eye's electroplate.

Blue next, from a coconut macaroon,
    the day-for-night
    filter you might
  look through to turn a sun into a moon.
That dog's a Quink hound now; the swing park is a ruin;
    the shrubs outside The Highwayman
    scratch up against the galleon
    pub-sign that's swinging in a wind
    straight out of Queen Anne's England,
and there's a general deepening, a thousand shades
    cast by the washing on the lines
that tacks hard like a navy in full sail.

    Lee, Wranglers, Fruit of the Loom
    restored to virginal denim,
    and midges in a streetlamp's glow
    are swirling like marine snow
at depths where light isn't supposed to go.
But too much blue is bad: it suffocates
    the senses to spend all your time
    in this sliver of the spectrum;
  and blue is precincts of celestial fate,
the concrete present flooded by eternal weight.

    Adding a yellow wrapper to
      the sheet of blue
  creates a green which covers everything,

a thousand years of growth at once,
our steady state, if given half a chance,
and you can hear birds sing.
Empire of moss and long barrow,
each doorway is an earth entrance
to *long ago* and *ever since*,
a source, Eurydice's hatch, a mammal burrow
that slows the eye and leads us down
into a sump where we could drown
happily, in a medium we've never known:
the future yet to rain, the past long flown.
But winter comes back harder, flesh falls from the bones

of trees whose flooded nests hang plain,
this novelty of looking drained
away, and which of us could say:
To morrow do thy worst, for I have liv'd to day . . .
Quinoline Yellow, Beta-carotene,
Allura Red, Riboflavin, Tartrazine,
you took us out of time and gave us power
to hype the moment, dye the day, and rob the hour.

Newts

The golf course pond where all ages collided.
The slime and larval casings of prehistory
but on hot days more a rococo mirror

from the swing in the trees. The silvering had gone
but we could fish fragile Kingeys and Queenies
out of its dark using newsagent nets

and study their webs and crests, their fronds and finery,
the English language mating without touching
in the shade of a hedge where we shrank from used sponkies.

I looked into the element of newts:
Knorr spring vegetable cold packet soup.
The same indefinite days we must all pass through.

And when the digger came we all brought jars
and worked quickly, in whispers, transplant surgeons
before that delicate kingdom dissolved.

The Airbrake People

You could drive a bus between each lonely gasp.
I listened through the night for steam-powered calls
between civic twilights, between songbirds,
a silence shared with shouts and breaking glass.

I pictured them as birds for a long time,
shy, cuspate creatures with the eyes of snakes
that haunted reed and marsh, ancient as light in the east,
at dusk coming among our streets and houses

the way an eddy of wind would worry the empties
and find a note so low it turned your bones
to milk. I'd count the minutes between each hiss:
all exhalation, nothing but dying fall

as if the night itself received a puncture,
as if there were a wounding in the dark.
They spoke to me. Or spoke to something in me.
And that's when I decided they were people,

a lost tribe come right to the edge of their woods.
I'd found signs in the bus stand and the car parks:
the funerary spoors of emptied ashtrays,
their hairclips and their little broken combs.

And none of this seemed stranger to me then
than finding ploughs or hunters in the sky,
or seeing Jack Frost in his suit of lights.
Something in me knew they were cold and starved.

One by one they were entering our clearing,
our blood-orange streetlight, our muddied dark,
so they could release those long, pneumatic sighs,
and that was how the airbrake people died.

Saturday Irons

Irons became attractive to the boys
who'd formerly paid them not the least attention,
except to spit on them when set to COTTON.
A scent hung in the hall: mainsails and sea-spray.
A bimetallic click. Things came to the boil

and so began the years of pressing creases
into a pair of slacks, or sharpening collars;
of green lights in the heels of ancient irons
meaning evenings were *on*; of fraying flexes
with a repeating diamond adder pattern;

the years of laying anchor with the plug
and dangling it like a lure so snarls
coiled up over the weeks wound themselves down;
of rusty shields scorched into shirts-for-school;
of irons, as heavy as a pint of bitter.

The lights clicked off. Things shrank. The schools burned down.
The shirts were grown out of. Those irons sank
like dead-weights where they'd once steamed full ahead
across the wrinkled fabric of the world,
into the kitchen cupboard's dark sea bed.

Digital

When I typed in 'Everything is happening all at once'
some saw a kind of rain, a smirr of ideas
that soaks us without knowing it, a downpour

on warm flagstones raising the ghost of our childhoods:
there were many channels. A runway's blizzard of banknotes
at the end of a heist movie, what the eyeball might clock

if shot from a cannon, the night sky brilliant
with the light arriving all at once. Others saw
themselves once and for all in a single moment

that blinded them, and they cried out to make it stop,
they wanted to get off, and some covered their ears
to block out the noise of everything happening all at once.

When I hit delete, snap my fingers, pull the plug,
you will open your eyes and see what's there. Now look:
it's only Victorian terraces, a row of allotments

being worked, a train slowing down on its approach
to the city, the various spires and chimneys of which
are still happening in grainy analogue.

Google Earth

Now I'm a hand setting the globe to spin,
finding a country, starting to zoom in
now I'm an eye. Now I'm a meteorite.

The scars of business corridors, the white
clay works, national parkland, estuaries.
A refinery built from Camemberts and Bries!

Now I'm a hand again, steadying my fall,
steering by starlight on the ground, black holes
of reservoirs, flight paths of major roads.

Now I'm an eye and there are never clouds
because the west wind of the Internet
blows silently down lost bus routes, birth streets,

the school roof still in bad need of repair,
the swing park all deserted at this hour,
which is no-hour. Now I'm the midnight sun

lighting the places where we've been and gone.
The ground comes up. A field sharpens to grain.
The trees screw into leaf. Now I'm a drop of rain.

Now I'm a balloon by Odilon Redon.
And now my chute snags up on power-lines.
If we looked outside, eyeballs might block the sun.

Even above the lake isles of Lough Gill,
Adlestrop's dismantled barrow, a hill
on the road north of Poughkeepsie, there are eyes

now all the world's a drop zone of the mind.

The Circling Stars

from the Anglo-Saxon

Five dozen reached the brink and pulled
their horses up (eleven spectrals,
four luminous whites). They'd trained for weeks
and were green to go, but this channel was tricky:
the swell a bastard, waves lit with foam,
the current strong. So the whole outfit
got scooped into a wagon, and under
the cosmic axle grease they rode, both
tooled-up man and horse, over
the waste to solid ground. No ox,
dray horse or slave sweat drew this wagon.
This was no sea or land haulage.
No feet got wet, all stayed airborne,
and there was no winding back, but by
degrees the wagon bore its load
from pick-up point to mount the shore
on the other side: so this brave squad crossed
the deeps and landed safely home.

The Planetarium

As my mind grows ever messier the planetarium
appeals more these days, with its simple clockwork dome
no higher than the mediaeval night, an horizon
cut by a silhouette artist, its crepuscular glow
that backlights this before the show, then drops us down
past dusk into darkest night – there is never a moon
and this sky is always cloudless – where constellations
wheel about the pole, and I throw my own shadows

up there: through the sped-up turning of the seasons
the planets track like headlamps across a ceiling;
I am carrying coal in from the shed, looking up
and seeing it all for the first time, or using a toothbrush
to spatter sugar paper with a Milky Way
of my own making; and when I look further back
am I seeing it all from a safe distance, the details
arranged about my own axis, giving order and meaning

to the night; and though I can still trick myself into thinking
I am looking down, as if into a monk's stock pond
or something deeper, that nothing pins me to this plush
but suggestion, or even leave *up* and *down* standing, to think
of me sitting just like this across the light-years
having these thoughts in two places at once; then why
am I always convinced by the pilot-light dawn that comes on
in a ring behind cut-out gasworks and tower blocks?

The Spoiler

The Spoiler wouldn't ever
reveal its ends to me.
Would never speak of rivers
flowing into the sea

or let slip how the boy
would get the girl. It said
that I should look away,
or cover my ears instead.

But then The Spoiler peeled
its gloves off, and I felt
the rough skin of the world
those silky hands had built.

The Cellar

Mind your head. The ceiling is low.
Slowly down the gritty steps
into the slower air of the cellar
past a ledge of tools and tins
of paint whose colours could be matched
upstairs, raised in a nick or scratch.

Following days of heavy rain
a chronic puddle reoccurs.
Its flagstones form a last attempt
at civilization. No coal comes now
but enough has fallen through this hole
to power the boilers of a ship.

The dark and damp stay anchored here
but fire once shared the room upstairs
with television. The utter disdain
the cellar must have felt for a world
where Callas' ear-ring or Ringo's snare
would catch the studio lights and flare

jet black across an ocean. Here,
a fathom below the floorboards,
in an agony of hooks and nails,
the colours peter out and stone
begins. Cobble and clay. Hard pan.
Below doesn't bear thinking about.

Moles

Within sight of the blue of the sky,
with meadow scents and the song of birds
as the gradient slackened, he looked back to find
more emptiness than he thought this earth

could hold. In this version of the myth
we leave him there, helpless and blind,
skimming for worms in the topsoil, cursed
with shovels that can't even hold a lyre.

Pop

Just as Beau Brummell's ferrule
and waistcoat have merged
with the wigs and stay-laces
of five decades earlier

in my mind, so the Ted
and the Mod and the Rocker
will slowly converge
in the fullness of time

to a mixture, an aggregate
post-war character
dug from a beach that
was once five miles inland,

the salt dark dissolving
the edges, the features,
till they can't tell between us
and none of it matters.

Gas

Seeing the country from a train
I've grown convinced its gasholders
in fact are used to house the spite
and gloom of post-industrial towns.

Arriving anywhere, I credit
them for signs, barometers
of bunkered call centres' black ids,
the rancour of each closing time.

Colourless and odourless
a leak betrays itself in a guard's
scowl, a strip-lit waiting room's
flicker. Whenever I do alight

each city reinventing itself
creaks like a warming glacier;
money, the old green-keeper,
has brought a springy, turf-like step

to the pavements but can't deal with gas.
Even on the leeward streets
the shoppers seethe and spend like mad.
Everybody wears a mask.

Cyan

I'm one of those model men
in barbershop or unisex
salon windows. I've held my breath
here, like this, for decades.

O distant youth, O brilliantine,
I saw myself the other day
across the street in running time:
gabardined, red-faced, gone grey.

The cow's-lick and the kiss curl.
I'm holding out. I'm blue in the face.
Telstar still orbits the Earth.
We don't like what you've done to the place.

Peter O'Sullevan

And the year Red Rum stole the Grand National at the
      long run in from The Elbow
I'm stood on the front at Blackpool with my back to the
      Illuminations
and though Irish poetry lies waiting in the future for me,
      I know
about Belfast over the dark water where these million
      bulbs don't shine,

and I know about myth, if myth is a mare and a sire, an
      Irish yard,
a momentous birth just a few days before my own, no
      photographers present
to record the event, then the runners and riders, and
      names on a meeting card
being identified out in the country in Peter O'Sullevan's
      winning accent

and his naval-issue binoculars might be trained on the
      frozen colours
of a heavenly object, 'and they cross the Melling Road' like
      the arm of a galaxy
and other great obstacles – The Elbow, The Chair,
      Valentine's Brook and Becher's –
could be train-set, scaled down versions of the pine-
      wooded hillsides of Mycenae,

and my aunt who lived in Aintree would turn the sound
        down on her telly
so we heard the hooves, the 'real horses', and something is
        gained and lost
years before I'll read a word of the verse which by fits and
        starts will lead me
to the Classical world, its stables and silks, but my wires
        are already crossed

and I'll always be thinking of spring in autumn, carrying
        different weights
through the world I've been given as well as the one that
        imaginatively obtains,
as a waterfall classically stilled when seen from a great
        distance at the height
of summer isn't ice, but a new way of thinking about
        Atlantic rain.

The Note Produced

The sixty-four-foot organ pipe,
the low C, shuddering *Jesus Christ*,
the engine room that makes cathedrals
dive, dive, dive, fathoms of flue

that drill into the bedrock, shift
knuckles and long bones in the crypt,

and you can feel the bottom line
right where the ribs all congregate,
a shiver trapped and brought to life.

The Dark Film

The dark film goes on general release.
Floodlights rake the low cloud base
above the scratchy London planes
and iron palings of Leicester Square.

Unrated dark, two hours long.
We wonder where the film was shot:
the *Night Mail* stopped, or *Empire State*
caught midway through a power cut,

or if they'd left the lens cap on
and gone with it, declared it 'art',
or if this were a film at all
or leader-tape blocking the light.

But something happens to the print
the further on into its run,
the further out each reel is sent:
audiences start seeing things.

An eyelash in Hitchin's Regal
grows four foot long, electrified,
a hairspring from a town-hall clock
in the screen's top right hand side

and in the Brighton Hippodrome
a pair of tracks cut by a bad
projector somewhere on the road
from Soho leaves them mesmerised

and by the time the film has reached
the oilrigs and the inset isles
it crackles like a bonfire
and radiant fibres twitch and turn

to thistledown and stars, scratches
to flak, to Dolby bumps felt in
the gut, a tracer fire of dust,
then faces, looked at long enough.

Brent Crude

Each one of us could fit inside a barrel,
assume foetal positions, elbows in,
suspended in the sweet and viscous black,
to dream our dreams as protean as plastics,
the petropounds on-stream and thick as blood
piped in from distant governmental rigs –
Heath, Wilson, Callaghan, Thatcher, Major –
and soundly sealed inside our private tar pits,
a reservoir, stockpiled in ziggurats
that none of us can know, knees to our chests,
could sleep the peacetime sleep, a colony
of seabirds bottled up and stacked on ledges,
a few waking to raise one useless wing
or open beaks up wide in silent protest.

The Milk Nostalgia Industries

When they send the fleet of floats into the dawn
you know they're trading in covert nostalgia.
When the empties tinkle and the motor strains
you know it's more than milk delivery.
The clean, reflective words *parlour* and *dairy*
can be squeezed for something far more nourishing.
Parlour in particular can yield
Jane Austen sitting on a milking stool
with a natty teat technique; that and a pail
each jet rings into, soft lit, in an English field.

And *dairy* draws on road maps' blank regions,
where sewage works and abattoirs and stud farms
exist as in original outlines
drawn up in Milk Nostalgia Head Office.
They say that down its corridors are rooms
where every bottled note left out is filed
before joining the archives underground.
Remember when we took the audio tour
to look upon this great, lost literature
writ in last-thing-at-night's forgotten hand?

Ah, the tour. The very milk of homesickness
was handed to us in warm tetra-paks,
and we felt our headphones fill with the white hiss
of the world speeding up. The milk turned black
as bull's blood, but before we reached the end
each saw their own arcades and galleries:
my father was down there, blowing on the skin
of boiling milk to calm its head of steam,
and my mother carrying a glass lit from within
to bed. And then the gift shop, full of cheese.

In the Wind

Gates go all Sergio Leone on me.
Waiters stand in doorways, under awnings
that lift like mainsails. All over the country
thousands of struck matches are sheltering
in practised hollows, passed on like secret handshakes.
It's the wind. It finds us out. I hear myself think

of Billy Gomez in the back of a Capri
with the windows down, as we drove to Anglesey
in nineteen eighty-two: 'Wind them fuckers up',
he croaked, 'I'm getting too much oxygen.'
I hear myself think of a Brixton room
five years later, the noise on my first night –

the hammering sash – then walking out at first light
into the litter left by the Great Storm
as if a carnival of the equinox
had passed through. It was nothing like the winds
in picture books, those faces made of vapour
puffing their cheeks, making weathervanes spin,

and whipping hats and bonnets from the heads
of flustered nineteen-fifties families.
It was like it always is. In my theory of wind
it stills us, or slows us down to thought.
I've always admired people who can sleep
in armchairs while a party blows itself out.

Odometer

Whatever way the tale is told –

– it always ends with a new owner
screwing open the odometer
all keen for winding back the clock
and finding there a folded note
which reads: *Oh no. Please. Not again.*
Or something else along those lines.

The surgeon lifts a heart from ice.
In the heat of his hands it begins to purr
like a bat being brought from a house at dusk,
and the way I always tell it, whoever
receives the heart feels ten years younger.
They only remember a blinding light

and a joke they must have heard when they were under.

Outside Cow Ark

Is mine the only heart out in this weather?
No. Grouse hearts beat in that turning heather.
Those midges scribbling patterns in late sun
fill their wings by dint of pinprick organs.
The privatized stream where I parked the car
contains trout hearts, idling in dead water.

Mine was switched on in another century,
in coal-fired rooms. Now other circuitry
that came online under this April's moon,
or cold hatches that sparked this very dawn,
is tuning one by one into my ancient valves.
The cardiac amperage hearts keep to themselves

links me up with livestock in the fold
but wilder blood-pumps out there must behold
a strange contraption, built for a long haul
far and away from home. The grouse will fall
before the year is done; the fish short out
inside a greater current; flies won't last the night.

Nostalgie Concrète

I'm ageing at the same increasing rate
but the years have bottled it, turned on their heels.
You've seen those films where pools come to the boil
then turn to glass as divers zip them shut,
feet first all the way back to the springboard;
you've seen Lancashire chimneys rise like trunks
of brick-dust mastodons, then stiffen up.
But living it? Listen. I'm one week in

and I never want to see a raindrop run
up a windowpane again, a biro drink
its words, or squatting dogs trained to insert
a link of turds. Eating out *is* eating out:
a string of unchewed bunting from the mouths
of people sobering up, re-entering coats
and leaving like an audience with the Queen
backwards into a night that's getting younger.

Though this isn't film. More the sun taking its light back,
coronal flares like bonfire sparks from each tree,
wall and face; more how mercury flows to the bright
elemental font. Looking back into that dark
I can see what's going to happen: friends go and come,
unsmoke more cigarettes and shed the pounds,
but mostly they'll forget. No one will see me
(each moment constantly undoes itself)

so I'll never meet them on the journey back
as they lose books, lighten up, and find the smiles
they didn't know they'd lost. And on the day
I die, an old ghost in 1971,
the sun will set in the east, the rain will rise
from pavements to the clouds, while all my friends
look through me with the wordless, wide-eyed stares
they were born with, as they head for home, feet first.

The Queen

We have a Queen. We're living in a Queendom.
This country has its best times under Queens.
She brings out all the bunting and the courtiers,
the peaceful demo and the strange headgear.

She is a fifties Queen in black-and-white
moving through the Commonwealth in newsreel;
a sixties Queen with a sister in the Bahamas;
a seventies Queen with a safety pin through her nose;

an eighties Queen eclipsed by a princess;
a nineties Queen advised not to lose touch.
(And I have never known anything different.)
She runs the House of Windsor as 'the Firm'.

If we work at it, the word 'queen' will abrade
to something strong and round and made of stone.
She does the regal wave from helicopters.
Her wrist orbit's a well-worn ball and socket.

On aerial views she is a great authority.
The landfill and the scars, the motorways,
the shrunken hunting grounds, the sea drawn back
to reveal the tidal extent of her realm.

I couldn't do it. Imagine waking up
in the blue silence of seven hundred rooms
in a palace in the middle of a city
and realising, *Jesus, I'm the fucking Queen!*

Ink

When *The Atlas of Ballistics & Projectiles*
was being prepared, we envied those who'd fuss
over the Ancient World, their fine lacework
of slingshot over buff washes of desert;
those who turned spear flights to scarlet tracks
through boreal greens; those who made Agincourt
look elegant, the aim of English longbows
and French archers embroidering the meadows

while we slaved on the Western Front, with all
its shadowless ordnance, where all our missiles
– from small bore to the grossest pig iron shell –
got lost each time we pulled them through the press,
the lines of fire so thick the colours bled
and slathered the plain of Picardy with mud.

Bridego Bridge

It's got nothing on the apple tree
where Newton had an idea or three.

It can't compete with the Kitty Hawk sand
where Orville left his shadow behind.

And it isn't like the Trinity site
where you could grub for some trinitite.

But under the bridge where the Train Robbers struck
time comes to a halt. It still wears the look

of dead Victorian housing stock
these days, and who will miss the brick

I wheedled from its stiff sentence
and have been questioning ever since:

You must have seen and heard it all.
Of course it's like talking to the wall.

The Snitch

In the final years of typewriters and memos
the old TV detectives are still being dragged in
to see their angry captains, who in turn
defend them to the D.A. and the Chief —
He is a maverick, but he gets results . . .
His methods are unusual, sure, I grant you . . .
Cicadas. Day-for-night shots. Then one actor
looks through the screen, out from his Californian
afternoon, as though he's seen the mirror in a brothel,

and even though he's in the simile business
this simile is giving him some trouble.
He prefers dipping his pinkie in the talcum
to lick the unadulterated stuff,
forcing confessions, clapping on the cuffs,
but he's looking right at you, out of character.
So come on twenty-first century, what can you tell him?

Creep

Shale rises a thousand feet
almost vertically; the sun
sets sometime shortly after noon.

Now the steam press of the cloud base
has put a tin lid on the day,

the lake darkening and darkening
as if a dye has been released

into us: toxin, tincture
crossing the blood–brain barrier,
the greyscale empire of slate.

But something else is happening
altogether vast and slow,

and as the light begins to go
we start to hear the scree, keeping
its stony, ancient time, ticking,

a kind of rock drizzle, the micro
readjustments of a clock

kept wound and running since the ice
retreated, and we feel the shock

of time in time, a pulse running
within the mainspring of a world
that keeps gaining and doesn't care.

Rapid Hardware

Seed and ore, onwards, towards
ruin and dross, and the hardware shop's

long pause, its hundred spirit levels
in stock, its silent lanes of timber,

its screw-drivers with long-shanks caught
in handles clear as Baltic amber,

its tacks and nails in swarm before
they leave to hold the world together,

its library of sandpaper
before it passes into scraps

and fragments, onwards, wrapped around
so many blocks of two-by-four;

and finding ourselves far from art
among these raw materials –

washers in the charity box,
unctions on high sunstruck shelves –

this is a proper place for prayer,
astringent turps and cross our hearts.

Boxer

Her face so grave and serious –
not the nettle-lick of the bulldog
or the irony of the pug –
as if she'd been bred to remind us

of the tenderness behind each tough
guy stance. I heard one brindled pup
spent a decade lashed to a nylon rope
in a garden next to an engine block,
another went down with kennel cough
and a third was kicked from the 79 bus

but ours stayed loved, and stoical.
After she died, the hole I dug
was so small, I had to break her leg
with the spade. She's giving me that look.

A Thousand Lines

Passing by your old school
spare a thought for lost blackboards,
the slow erosion and tap of chalk
that notated long afternoons.

Lost desks engraved with biro ink,
carved with nicknames, a marquetry
of gum, the coarse anatomy
of skewered hearts and spurting dicks.

But the window hook must still be there:
the highest panes are open wide.
The kids are doing synthetic phonics.
The lesson drifts into the air.

They should have had you stay behind
and made you write a thousand lines.
I will not write nostalgic poems.
I will put these things out of mind.

The Mind

Asleep, the organs form a line to see
the mind. The liver won't stand for much more,
so the mind issues a warning in the form
of a sad dream that will haunt it through the day.

The kidneys do their double-entry audit,
the same old calculations: the mind has heard it
ten thousand times, but feigns interest and calm.
This number crunching can't do any harm.

The spleen reminds the mind that in the death
it will stay open longest of them all,
remaining at its post, admitting cells
to a party gone cold, past each lung's last breath,

beyond the heart's much vaunted in-and-out.
But the mind reminds the spleen 'glorified pump'
is out-of-line; that it must learn to let
go of the heart's cruel 'overrated sump'.

Let go. Forgive. Fall into line. Move on.
The mind repeats itself. When all is said
and done, as the last gland shuffles out at dawn,
tired, the mind comes to the bit it dreads.

Brawn

Anonymous cows and pigs from another century,
chewing and rooting under fizzing pylons,
enter my head, in another country,
after a day of dusty shade and strong sun;

after so many relics, frescoes, altars,
I think of Lancashire's lost herds and flocks
when a waiter brings us *testa in cassetta*
which, in another tongue, means 'head in a box'.

Now shuttling through the slicer, back and forth,
a loaf of brawn, big as a pulpit bible.
The blade is set so fine the leaves that fall
onto the butcher's newsprint leave it legible.

Each shaving like a pane of pink stained-glass
that told brawn's story. Animals translated
by bolt, by block, by scales, and always one of us
writing our name in sawdust while we waited.

Cloaca Maxima

I

Sewer-jumping in a childhood twilight
the boy looks up a moment and feels something.
Water thick as Bovril doesn't move.
There's a holding of the breath in a concrete outfall.
It's an ear-to-the-rail moment,
or pipe-work, leading back to God-knows-where,
before an iron door slams shut on the splendours.

II

Moment containing all the fine escapees
of history, crawling through the dark, emerging
from unmarked graves aligned to navigations
they dug and died alongside. One long chain gang
raised from tobacco fields unlocked from work-songs
they sung in warmer, thicker air – *If you
Don't believe I'm a sinkin, look what a hole I'm in* –
the blistered of the Dismal Swamp Canal
who've travelled via the Underground Railroad
and Anacharsis Cloots – what's he doing here?
– with Representatives of the Human Race
all covered in shit, blinking in the light of day,
the shut-in, nameless multitudes, the lost bones,
the leg-irons and the long shanks and the ledger-
entered of Goree Island: all raised up!

III

Look at these three, marching through the visible field
from left to right, a ragged and sooty sentence
in the buttery, limestone light, in the middle of a century.
Marching into three futures long since past.

The little one says to the big one: *Who is this bloke?*
in a lost vernacular of Parisian sweeps
which the camera couldn't record. To which the big one
replies: *Never mind. Keep looking straight ahead*

though he's secretly intrigued. The apparatus
is a little like when a chimney grate's sealed off
by a canvas rig. And how many days has he seen
as a pinprick at the end of a carbon flue?

The middle one has climbed towards this light
so many times already in his short life,
and you want to tell him how long he's lasted in it
where so many others are shut in the dusty dark.

IV

Or think in terms of a movie shot
on a shoestring, where the eye is drawn
to the extras who are swapping hats
and passing by again and again.

Only replace its flimsy set
with sewers and ditches and holes in the ground,
and a scene that lasts millions of feet;
and the background babble with the sound

of a bullwhip that reverberates
down dark tunnels, and the same faces
come round eventually if you wait
for a few lifetimes and remain in your places.

V

The sleepers' hands are put to work.
Workhouse children unsnarl looms
and sharecroppers shuck peas from pods
and cocklers rake through dark mortar
and cotton pickers twist the buds
and bonded women solder boards
and run the fabric through the foot
and guide it down the miles of seam
and punkah wallahs pull the cord
and galley rowers bend through oars
and railroad workers tap the rails
and drainage diggers heft the spade
and all of this and so much more
is happening in the place of dreams.
The sleepers' hands are put to work.

VI

And this is what the boy has seen: the dreams
kept hidden, either by great distances
or the pearlescent blind eye that we need
to grow to keep the world under our noses
safely removed. The millions of mixed shades
are still running beneath our surfaces
and visible to those who just step sideways
anywhere: a city square at dusk,
a sun-warmed wall asking to have an ear
lent to its crumbling roughcast, old outfalls
like this one, where a boy gave way to thought
thirty years ago, on a backfield, in the north.

Big Fish

It's like returning to a natal pool
after years of doing business in great waters,
and only a few will make it whole,
the dreams of youth unsullied and intact
after all they've seen in the world's working mirrors,
its splendid distractions, the weight of its cold hard facts,

and the driver lets you off at the foot of the hill
and you pass the substation humming its old song
about power being stepped down, the climbing frame
in the swing-park posing its puzzle, and before long
your birth street greets you with an ambush of smells:
teatimes in doorways where no-one remembers your name.

The Circuit

I want to be laid to rest in a substation.
I want the padlocked door I tried for hours
as a bored and disrespectful child to be swung open;
to be placed respectfully next to transformers.

These will hum to me in the quiet after you've gone.
The gravel that my brick mausoleum stands in
is freshly raked, but soon teasels and docks
will grow waist high, and I want this to happen.

Lying in the dark river of flux
I want to feel the increased demand of autumn
in a frantic tittle-tattle of switching gear.
Between the power station and our home

I want to lie and abide and bridge the gap
so you might think of me as the days shorten;
a little shock each time you find you're sat
in the dark, and rise to put the big light on.

Acknowledgements

Many thanks to the editors of the following publications, in which some of these poems first appeared: the *Edinburgh Review*, *Five Dials*, *GQ*, *Granta*, *Harper's Magazine*, *Manhattan Review*, *Matter*, *Poetry London*, *Poetry Review*, the *Spectator*, the *Times Literary Supplement*.

A version of 'Peter O'Sullevan' can be found in *From the Small Back Room: a Festschrift for Ciaran Carson* (Netherlea Press); 'Cloaca Maxima' was first published in *I Have Found a Song* (Enitharmon Press); 'The Circling Stars' was commissioned as a version of Riddle 22 from the Exeter Book, included in *The Word Exchange: Anglo-Saxon Poems in Translation* (Norton), and I'd like to thank Michael Matto for his help during the crossing.